The Ruskin Lecture
Mappin Art Gallery, Sheffield, 10

RUSKIN AND SHEFFIELD

The Museum of The Guild of St George
and its making

Robert Hewison

Published by
The GUILD of ST GEORGE

The Ruskin Lecture 1979
First published 1981 for The Guild of St George by Brentham Press, London

ISBN 0 905772 06 7

Revised edition published 2011 by The Guild of St George

ISBN 978-0-9554469-8-6

Reprinted 2013

The Guild of St George
Publications secretary: Peter Miller,
10 St Oswald's Road, York YO10 4PF

www.guildofstgeorge.org.uk

Cover: John Wharlton Bunney (1828-1882)
Western Façade of the Basilica of San Marco, Venice.
Oil on canvas, painted between 1877-1882
145 x 226cm. Ruskin Collection Sheffield

Printed by Reptotech Studio Ltd, York YO1 6EL

FORWORD

A version of this account of the making of the Museum of the Guild of St George first appeared as the 1979 Guild of St George Ruskin Lecture "Art and Society: Ruskin in Sheffield 1876", and was published for the Guild by the Brentham Press. The times, and the circumstances of the Guild's collection, have much altered since 1979, and I have taken the opportunity to revise and expand my text, and to bring the history of the collection briefly up to date.

The Guild of St George does many good things; one of the most important of them is to ensure that this material link between Ruskin's ideas and values and the City of Sheffield that the Museum of the Guild of St George represents remains intact. I am very grateful to the present Master of the Guild, Clive Wilmer, and his predecessor, James Dearden, for their help in reviving this narrative of a noble venture.

Robert Hewison
February 2011

ART AND SOCIETY: RUSKIN IN SHEFFIELD 1876

ON Friday, 28 April 1876, the following report appeared on page three of the *Sheffield Daily Telegraph*:

MR RUSKIN IN SHEFFIELD

COMMUNISM AND ART

Last evening, about twenty persons assembled at the New Museum established by Mr Ruskin, at Walkley, for the purpose of hearing Mr Ruskin's opinions on various subjects, and of giving their own. Amongst those present were six ladies. The proceedings were chiefly of a conversational nature, and no set speech on any one of the several subjects dealt with was given. Primarily, the subject of Communism came up, and its most extreme principles were freely and enthusiastically advocated by one or two of those present.[1]

This newspaper account is among the earliest public recognitions of John Ruskin's association with Sheffield. The event reported was one of the first manifestations of Ruskin's practical work for the radical, utopian society that he was in the process of forming, the Guild of St George, and it records the beginnings of an important connection between the Guild and Sheffield that continues to this day.

As seen though the eyes of a local reporter, who knew how to insert a touch of irony into his writing, Ruskin does not come off very well. Sent up to the hilltop suburb of Walkley to cover an obscure meeting in an obscure cottage with no more commitment than if he had been sent to cover a bankruptcy hearing, a meeting of the Sheffield School Board, or of shareholders in the Kelham Rolling Mills Company Ltd – all of which appear on the same page as his account of Walkley – the reporter must have been bemused to observe this encounter between one of the leading public intellectuals of the day, and a group of enthusiastic 'communists' – and six ladies.

The social and aesthetic message that Ruskin had been preaching since the publication of *The Stones of Venice* in 1851-53, most explicitly in *Unto This Last* (1860), tended to be greeted with suspicion. When his decision to found a museum intended to enlighten the lives of working-class people in Sheffield was announced in 1875, the *Sheffield Portrait Gallery: a journal of literature, criticism and satire* published this snobbish comment from 'Barnaby Braggs', in his column 'Jottings on my Thumbnail':

Mr Ruskin is bent upon improving the people of Sheffield, by a museum which he is to fit up to his own liking. The greatest curiosity he could exhibit would be – himself.[2]

The period 1875-6 was very important in the history of the Guild of St George, and for Ruskin's proposals for social reform generally. It was the moment when a theoretical discussion of his ideas began to give way to their application in reality. What the anonymous report for the *Sheffield Daily Telegraph* gives us is a real Ruskin, in a real room. And a cramped and small one it turned out to be.

* * *

Ruskin's principal medium for promoting his ideas on reform in art and society was the publication *Fors Clavigera*, his monthly personal newsletter – the Victorian equivalent of a blog – addressed to the 'workmen and labourers of England', which he had launched in January 1871. It was published and distributed by his assistant, George Allen, a former joiner whom Ruskin had recruited from his drawing classes for the London Working Men's College in the 1860s. (It helped that Allen had married Ruskin's mother's maid.) Running in parallel with *Fors Clavigera* were Ruskin's lectures as the first Slade Professor of Fine Art at Oxford University.

Although there is plenty of art matter in *Fors Clavigera*, and plenty of social criticism in the Oxford lectures, the appeal to the public in *Fors Clavigera* was chiefly of a social nature. *Fors Clavigera* was the vehicle through which he promoted the practical application of his ideas: first in the shape of the St George's Fund, which was intended to buy up waste land and make it fruitful – a fund which he established with the gift of one tenth of his shrinking personal fortune. This developed into the St George's Company, a group of people who would assist this social and environmental project in various ways, with money or voluntary work. When legal difficulties prevented the use of the word 'Company' – the Board of Trade would not register a company that did not intend to make a profit – this became the Guild of St George, with a legal constitution appointing trustees, Ruskin as 'Master', a membership and a formal function. One of its responsibilities, when the Guild finally acquired a proper legal identity in 1878, was to own and administer the Museum at Walkley that had been brought into existence early in 1876.

While *Fors Clavigera* enabled Ruskin to promote his practical scheme for art and social reform, it is important to understand what these monthly letters really were. As Ruskin himself wrote:

> *Fors is a letter*, and written as a letter should be written, frankly, and as the mood, or topic, chances; so far as I finish and retouch it, which of late I have done more and more, it ceases to be what it should be, and becomes a serious treatise, which I never meant to undertake.[3]

The letters are a way of talking to people, or better, of arguing with them. As he said in one of the earliest numbers: 'I neither wish to please, nor displease you; but to provoke you to think' (27.99). As the popularity – or notoriety – of *Fors Clavigera* grew, people began to write to Ruskin, agreeing with him, or answering back, and hence a sort of correspondence column started to appear at the end of each monthly number. It is from these correspondents, including the few who actually sent money to the St George's Fund, that the membership of the Guild of St George grew.

As we know, personal discussions and arguments take a rather different shape from the formalised statements of public debate, and even in debate the demands of rhetoric or the heat of the moment can lead to statements that would look absurd if printed in the chill print of a book – or a newspaper report. *Fors Clavigera* is the voice of Ruskin in conversation, and it has all the tones that we would expect to hear in a dialogue: reminiscences, anecdote, bits out of the newspaper, humour, delight, teasing, satire, discussion, argument, anger, and, at the top of the scale, fierce polemic. We hear about Ruskin's schemes for the Guild of St George in these tones of voice, but rarely in the single authoritative voice of command. As Ruskin says: '*Fors Clavigera* contains not a plan or scheme, but a principle and tendency' (28.227).

Fors had been running for five years when Ruskin came to Walkley in 1876, and in spite of the jibes of the newspapers, who always found it good for a joke, it was building up a following. On 20 February 1876 its publisher, George Allen, wrote to another of Ruskin's occasional assistants, also recruited from the Working Men's College, the painter J. W. Bunney:

> *Fors* is getting popular and we shall issue the full thousand per month of the current number, besides the back ones – you would be surprised at the number of bound sets we sell now – bound volumes'.[4]

The 'principle and tendency' of *Fors* was towards practical work, and by the beginning of 1876 the St George's scheme had received fifty-four subscriptions to the Fund, and twenty of the donors had been accepted into what would become the Guild as Companions. It had also acquired responsibility for seven acres of woodland in Bewdley, Worcestershire (later growing to twenty) given by the Birmingham local politician George Baker, and a small group of cottages at Barmouth in Wales, given by Ruskin's friend Mrs Fanny Talbot. It also owned the cottage and property at Bellhagg Road, Walkley, Sheffield, which held the nucleus of the Museum of the Guild of St George.

Agriculture and museums may seem an odd combination of responsibilities for a single organisation, but the land and the museum collection are the polarities of Ruskin's unified scheme. In between – at least in theory – lay an elaborate social organisation, a society that would present a radical alternative to the structure of the contemporary world. The basis of this society was agriculture, for according to Ruskin's economic principles, as laid down in *Unto This Last*, labour was the only source of value. Only manual labour had dignity, which meant that steam engines and sewing machines were banned from Guild land. Members of the Guild were organised in a strict hierarchy, with a Master elected by an aristocracy of members. The Master was to have absolute authority over the Guild's affairs, although he could be deposed by a majority of the Companions. He was to be assisted by Marshals; below them came landlords, land agents, tenantry, tradesmen, and hired labourers; while outside the Guild there would be an 'irregular cavalry' of friends (28.424). In contrast to the Bishops of the Church of England there would be an episcopal system by which Bishops of the Guild really oversaw and were responsible for the moral and physical welfare of every member – and acted as a kind of police force in financial matters.

Not all members of the Guild would work full-time on the Guild's schemes, for it was not intended as a retreat from the world, but rather, members would be 'a band of delivering knights' (28.538). Ruskin had wanted to call it a Company because that was the name given to the companies of mercenaries that had fought in Italy in the sixteenth century, but as we have seen, that was not acceptable to the Board of Trade (28.628-9). There were to be three classes of members of the Guild: 'Companions Servant', who worked mainly for the Guild, with some private interests; 'Companions Militant' who worked full-time, such as agricultural workers; and 'Companions Consular' who gave one tenth of their income to the Guild, but carried on their normal occupations while following St George's principles (28.539). Ruskin later dropped the requirement that Companions should give one tenth of their income.

Because the capitalist system had created nothing but a National Debt, the Guild's purpose was to create a 'National Store':

> The possession of such a store by the nation would signify, that there were no taxes to pay; that everybody had clothes enough, and some stuff laid by for next year; that everybody had food enough, and plenty of salted pork, pickled walnuts, potted shrimps, or other conserves, in the cupboard; that everybody had jewels enough, and some of the biggest laid by, in treasuries and museums; and, of persons caring for such things, that everybody had as many books and pictures as they could read or look at; with quantities of the highest quality besides, in easily accessible public libraries and galleries (28.641).

* * *

The museum, then, was a manifestation of this delightful, generous conception of a National Store. But it also had an educational purpose, for land and farms meant people, and so a comprehensive system of education was necessary. The children of the Guild's labourers or 'Companions Militant' would be taught in:

> agricultural schools inland, and naval schools by the sea, the indispensable first condition of such education being that the boys learn either to ride or to sail; the girls to spin, weave, and sew, and at a proper age to cook all ordinary food exquisitely; the youth of both sexes to be disciplined daily in the strictest practice of vocal music; and for morality, to be taught gentleness to all brute creatures, – finished courtesy to each other, – to speak truth with rigid care, and to obey orders with the precision of slaves (27.143).

The children would be taught with the aid of teaching examples, such as those he had provided for the School of Drawing that he had recently founded at Oxford.

The teaching system extended into the Companions' homes, for each was to have a *Bibliotheca Pastorum*, a cottage library of standard volumes edited and published by the Guild (28.20). There would also be a standard collection of works of art available for each house. This educational scheme, like the elaborate constitutional scheme for the Guild, was never put into practice, nor even fully worked out. For instance, at one stage he proposes that the boys and girls of the Guild should be taught Latin, elsewhere he says that they should not be taught to read or write at all. But one fragment of the scheme, an educational museum, did come into existence, at Walkley.

But why Walkley, and why Sheffield? There is what might be called an official, and an unofficial, reason for this. The official reason was given by Ruskin in his *General Statement explaining the Nature and Purposes of St George's Guild*, issued in 1882:

> I am now frequently asked why I chose Sheffield for it – rather than any other town. The answer is a simple one – that I acknowledge Ironwork as an art always necessary and useful to man, and English work in iron as masterful of its kind . . . . Not for this reason only, however, but because Sheffield is in Yorkshire, and Yorkshire yet, in the main temper of its inhabitants, old English, and capable therefore of the ideas of Honesty and Piety by which Old England lived; finally, because Yorkshire is within easy reach of beautiful natural scenery, and of the best art of English hands, at Lincoln, York, Durham, Selby, Fountains, Bolton, and Furness (30.51-52).

Complimentary as these reasons are, and not disputing Ruskin's deserved remarks about the good people and fine scenery of Yorkshire, there was also a more direct reason for the choice of Sheffield as a location.

The timing of Ruskin's social appeal, and his attempt to put his ideas into practice, must be seen in the context of the 1870s, which saw the first stirrings of the reawakened radical movements of 1848, expressed in the formation of political groups, charitable settlements and utopian communities. Sheffield had a strong radical tradition, both in terms of religious dissent and of political memories that went back to the Chartists and the Sheffield Corresponding Society. It was a fruitful soil for those who wanted to cultivate social change, as the early socialist Edward Carpenter discovered when he moved to Sheffield in 1878. As Sheila Rowbotham has pointed out in her book on Carpenter: 'The communitarian tradition had never really died in the Sheffield area, perhaps because a structure of small workshop production and small holdings persisted'.[5]

It still required, however, someone to plant the particular seed of Ruskin's ideas in this well-prepared soil. That person was Henry Swan.

The links between Ruskin and Henry Swan go back to 1855, when Ruskin was teaching drawing at the London Working Men's College, in its early days in Red Lion Square. Swan was one of his pupils, and like others he taught, became a cross between an assistant and a disciple. Born in Devizes in 1825, Swan was what can only be described as a 'character'. He served an apprenticeship to a copper-plate engraver; at the Working Men's College he took a particular interest in the illumination of manuscripts, being employed at one time by Ruskin to copy manuscripts in the British Museum. In the 1850s he became a Quaker, and according to one of his obituarists this conversion was all the more remarkable for having been the result of his devotion to art and music, something treated with suspicion by some of the more serious-minded Friends.[6] Swan's interests were manifold, as this reminiscence records:

> He invented what was considered at the time an important improvement to photography. He was also the parent of a method of musical notation, and had perfected a system of phonetic spelling. He was also one of the first to introduce the now familiar bicycle into this country, and at another time made an attempt to popularise the throwing of the boomerang.[7]

Henry Swan was also a shorthand expert, a vegetarian, and, something that Ruskin's editors Cook and Wedderburn chose not mention, a Spiritualist.[8]

With no disrespect to Spiritualists, vegetarians and throwers of the boomerang, it appears that Swan was something of a crank, and 'crank' is precisely the word that George Allen used of him after his death.[9] But Ruskin put his trust in him, at least to begin with, and made him the first Curator of the Guild Museum, on a salary of £40 a year. Writing to his solicitors, Tarrant and Mackrell, and of course anxious to impress on them Swan's trustworthiness, Ruskin describes Swan as: 'an honest, though somewhat dreamy person . . . [he is] very poor and has never asked me for money'.[10] Swan had settled in Sheffield in order to pursue his trade as an engraver – Ruskin says he was working 'on plated goods or silver';[11] in August 1875 Ruskin gives his address as 33 Times Buildings, Bow Street, Sheffield.[12] By September 1875, however, it had become Bellhagg Road, Walkley.

* * *

Ruskin's immediate connections with Sheffield can be traced through the somewhat sketchy entries in his diary. The key time is the year preceding the visit of April 1876. On 26 January 1875 he passed through the Sheffield area on a posting tour, having made the somewhat eccentric decision to travel in the old fashioned way in a carriage driven by a postillion, changing horses along the way. He was again in Sheffield on 3 July, although there is no indication that he stopped for long there. But Ruskin and Swan were already in correspondence about his plans for the Guild, and the vital entry in his diary is for 5 July: 'Pleasant letter from Sheffield to be answered'.[13] On 12 July he wrote to Swan:

> It is very wonderful to me the coming of your letters just at this time. The chief point in my own mind in material of education is getting a museum, however small, well explained and clearly and easily seen. Can you get with any Sheffield help, a room with good light, anywhere accessible to the men who would be likely to come to it? If so, I will send you books and begin with minerals of considerable variety and interest, with short notes on each specimen, and others of less value, of the same kinds which the men may examine and handle at their ease.[14]

The idea of an educational museum as part of the work of St George was about to become a reality, for on 18 July he wrote again to Swan that he was prepared to negotiate for a site for the museum.

On 26 and 27 September 1875 Ruskin came to Sheffield, staying at the Royal Hotel, specifically to see Swan. The important phrase in the letter just quoted is 'the men'. It is evident that Swan was the leader, or member, of a group of Sheffield working men interested in social reform. On 26 September, the day of his arrival, Ruskin wrote to his cousin and companion Joan Severn:

> I've seen my quaker friend and am going to lunch with him and have a talk with the men he wishes me to know of the Sheffield operatives but I shall not be back in time to tell you anything this evening.[15]

And he was not, so we do not know exactly what took place, apart from an entry in his diary for 27 September: 'I went up to Walkley and talked to workmen and returned, somewhat wearied, in gloomy wreck of watery sunset'.[16]

What we do know is that on the same day he wrote to his solicitors telling them to buy the cottage and land in Bellhagg Road, Walkley. The property was owned by the Rivelin View Society, one of the dozen building societies developing the Nether Hallam area, and the purchase, for £600, was completed on 10 November. On 3 November Swan had been offered the post of curator. We can thank the reporter of the *Sheffield Daily Telegraph* for his account of what happened when Ruskin next came to Sheffield, on 27 April 1876, to see what progress had been made. The 'new museum' the reporter describes was not as grand as the phrase suggests. It was in fact a small stone-built cottage, surrounded by a small orchard, in which Henry Swan, his wife, and his son Howard (and possibly another son, who later settled in Florida) were also living. This time Ruskin had brought Joan Severn and her husband, the minor painter and son of Keats's friend, Arthur Severn, along for the trip, staying at the King's Head. They were making a holiday of it, on another posting tour, for which he had had a carriage especially built. (The carriage can be seen today at Ruskin's Lake District home, Brantwood, Coniston.) Arthur Severn wrote later that he remembered:

1. The Museum of the Guild of St George, c.1876. The earliest known photograph of the upper room of the cottage at Walkley.

2. The Museum of the Guild of St George, c.1885. The original cottage has been extended to the rear to accommodate a growing collection.

> the look of regret on the Professor's [Ruskin's] face when he saw how cramped the space was there for the things he had to show. However, with his usual kindness, he did not say much about it at the time, and he did not complain about the considerable amount of room it was necessary for the curator and his family to take up in that place.[17]

In view of the smallness of the room, the turnout of twenty persons (including six ladies) that the reporter records seems impressive.

* * *

Having learnt why Ruskin chose Sheffield, the next question is why Sheffield – or the twenty persons who came to Walkley – should chose to hear Ruskin. The answer lies in the headline to the *Telegraph* report: 'Communism and Art'. As the reporter writes, there were a number of people in the room who called themselves Communists. Whatever they understood by the word Communist, they were among the first of many to mistake the true direction in which Ruskin's politics lay.

The source of this misunderstanding is probably the seventh number of *Fors Clavigera*, for July 1871, where he does indeed describe himself as a Communist: 'of the old school – reddest also of the red' (27.116). But Ruskin's Communism was of a more domesticated kind. The three laws of Communism, he writes, are firstly: 'everybody must work in common, and do common or simple work for his dinner' (27.117). The second principle concerns property:

> it is that the public, or common, wealth shall be more and statelier in all its substance than private or singular wealth; that is to say (to come to my own special business for a moment) that there shall be only cheap and few pictures, if any, in the insides of houses, where nobody but the owner can see them; but costly pictures, and many, on the outsides of houses, where the people can see them (27.120).

Finally, Ruskin says, it is an absolute law:

> that the fortunes of private persons should be small, and of little account in the State; but the common treasure of the whole nation should be of superb and precious things in redundant quantity, as pictures, statues, precious books, gold and silver vessels, preserved from ancient times; gold and silver bullion laid up for use, in case of any chance need of buying anything suddenly from foreign nations; noble horses, cattle, and sheep, on the public lands; and vast spaces of land for culture, exercise and garden, round the cities, full of flowers, which, being everybody's property, nobody could gather; and of birds which, being everybody's property, nobody could shoot (27.121).

These quotations abbreviate an argument of several pages, but it is plain that if this is Communism, it is of an unfamiliar and particularly aesthetic kind. As a statement of principles, it is at least more coherent than one made by a member of his audience at Walkley, who, the reporter noted: 'gave his idea of what a state a Communism ought to be. They should all live together in furnished apartments, and they should start at the outset by manufacturing boots' (30.307). To which Ruskin replied – why not hats?

The reason, in July 1871, that Ruskin should call himself a Communist 'of the old school' – and that phrase is significant – is that the whole number of *Fors* is set in the context of contemporary events in France. The word Communist had a certain resonance in view of the uprising known as the Commune from March to May in Paris that year. From the very first number of *Fors*, the Franco-Prussian war, the siege of Paris and the uprising by the communards that followed played an important part in his arguments, as facts in themselves, and as an example of the follies of the industrial age. For the government and the people of Paris to follow on the defeat by falling on one another – and setting fire to the Louvre in the process – was an extension of this tragedy. Ruskin responds to these events by presenting himself as an 'old' Communist, and his principles of co-operation and common wealth are set down in contrast to those in operation in Paris. It is Ruskin being polemical, adopting an extreme position in order to turn the argument inside out. He is also teasing – were it not for his underlying seriousness.

During his visit to Sheffield in 1876 Ruskin reaffirmed: 'as to "Communism", that he believed in it in its broad principles, and had so far advocated it. The word Communism was susceptible of many meanings' (30.307). In Ruskin's case that was certainly true, for immediately after the 'communist' number of *Fors* appeared, Ruskin wrote to one of the Trustees of St George's Fund, the senior civil servant William Cowper-Temple: 'It is *not* to be *Communism*: quite the contrary. The old Feudal system applied to do good instead of evil – to save life, instead of destroy. That is the whole – in fewest words'.[18] This version of the purpose of the Guild gives a clue to the real source of Ruskin's vision.

Because of Ruskin's contradictory statements – all part of his polemical technique – Ruskin's politics have seemed evasive, even when he has made the most overt declarations of his beliefs. In the first number of *Fors* Ruskin had made his independence from party politics clear:

> As you would find it thus impossible to class me justly in either party, so you would find it impossible to class any person whatever, who had clear and developed political opinions, and who could define them accurately. Men only associate in parties by sacrificing their opinions, or by having none worth sacrificing; and the effect of party government is always to develop hostilities and hypocrisies, and to extinguish ideas (27.15).

Nonetheless, there is one statement that can be taken at face value – the one that opens his autobiography *Praeterita*: 'I am, and my father was before me, a violent Tory of the old school' (35.13).

The more than a hundred of years party government, whose principles Ruskin so despised, have, since he made this statement, so changed the meaning of political labels, that it is surprising to discover what Ruskin meant by 'a violent Tory of the old school'. The 21st century Tory party would exclude him, on the grounds that he rejected their economic liberalism and blind faith in the market; the Labour party would reject him on the grounds that he did not believe in universal suffrage. In fact, Ruskin, and his father, John James Ruskin, supported a wing of the Tory party that was already disappearing in the 1850s, the Ultra-Tories. As their name implies, the Ultra-Tories had never reconciled themselves to the Great Reform Act of 1832, nor to the Catholic emancipation that had preceded it. They believed in a strictly hierarchical society, with limited suffrage, and the exclusion from power of all those who were not members of the Church of England: the Church and the Crown being identified as the joint guarantors of English society. In economics they were fundamentally anti-capitalist, they abhorred Free Trade, and favoured interventionist measures such as the Corn Laws.

The Ultra-Tory party was closely identified with the Evangelical wing of the Church of England, and indeed drew most of its intellectual support from there. Ruskin began his career as an Evangelical intellectual, and the Ruskin family was friendly with a number of Ultra-Tory churchmen. Nor were the Ultra-Tories without economic theoreticians, who in *Blackwood's Edinburgh Magazine* put forward a coherent economic philosophy. One such was David Robinson who, incidentally, signed himself 'One of the Old School'.

In a series of articles for *Blackwood's* in 1829 and 1830 Robinson put forward a number of principles that are remarkably similar to Ruskin's practice in the Guild of St George. Not only was Robinson in favour of a hierarchy and harmony of social classes – Ruskin's 'old Feudal system applied to do good rather than evil' – in particular he was concerned about the problem of waste land. Robinson argued that an increase in agricultural employment would lead to an increase in industrial employment, to the general benefit of the nation. Since all the good land was already in use, the land lying idle and in need of improvement must be brought under cultivation. To this end he advocated a state scheme that would put up the capital for drainage and other work, and divide the land into allotments of from ten to a hundred acres, the smallest holding being available to those who wished to support themselves while carrying out another trade. It is remarkable, in the context of the Guild of St George, that Robinson should comment: 'To the plan for establishing the poor on waste land by means of societies, I am a warm friend'.[19]

* * *

In typical Ruskinian fashion, we have moved from museums to agriculture, but in true Ruskinian manner, they are intimately connected, for one of the results of the 1876 visit to Sheffield was an agricultural scheme. The bringing into cultivation of land, specifically waste land, was one of the declared principles of the Guild of St George. (Drainage, in particular, was almost an obsession of Ruskin's.) In his earliest sketch of the Guild scheme, in the fifth number of *Fors*, for May 1871, Ruskin says: 'I do not care with how many, or how few, this thing is begun, nor on what inconsiderable scale, – if it be but in two or three poor men's gardens. So much, at least, I can buy, myself, and give them' (27.95-6). And, lest there should be any doubt as to his authoritarianism, while he proposes to: 'take some small piece of English ground, beautiful, peaceful, and fruitful' (27.96), he also outlines the political system that will prevail there:

> We will have no liberty upon it; but constant obedience to known law, and appointed persons: no equality upon it; but recognition of every betterness that we can find, and reprobation of every worseness (27.96).

Shortly after his visit to Sheffield in 1876, Ruskin found himself doing precisely what he had proposed, buying some land for poor men to cultivate. This was the thirteen-acre farm just across the county border with Derbyshire, in Totley. At first, Ruskin preferred to use the prettier name of Abbeydale. Since the Guild did not yet have a legal identity, he was obliged to buy the farm in his own name, and the tenants were not members of the Guild. They were in fact some of the working men gathered around Henry Swan. A single sheet of paper in the Guild's archives, unfortunately undated, lists the names and addresses of sixty 'working men', together with some fifty names and addresses of professional people under the heading 'List for communications (not working)'. Besides these lists, which would be of great interest to a local historian, there is a third, headed 'Candidates for Abbeydale', and giving a dozen names and addresses, some of them drawn

3. St George's Farm, Totley, probably in post-communist days.

from the list of working men. Henry Swan's skill in shorthand came in useful – for it is almost certainly his list. There are comments in shorthand on the families and characters of the 'candidates'; no fewer than four are noted as bootmakers, and it is possible that the earnest Communist who wished to reach that ideal state by living in furnished apartments, had hopes of working at Totley.

The Totley scheme matches the proposals of David Robinson in that the idea was that the land should be used as allotments, and, if not exactly waste, it was certainly poor land, so poor that the two trustees of the St George's Fund resigned in protest at the purchase. The scheme was not a success. The land was bad, the men had little agricultural experience, and fell out with each other. Ruskin commented in *Fors* for November 1877:

> The root of all mischief is of course that the Master is out of the way, and the men, in his absence, tried at first to on get by vote of the majority; – it is at any rate to be counted as no small success that they have entirely convinced themselves of the impossibility of getting on in that popular manner (29.273).

Ruskin may have derived some satisfaction from this failure of democracy, but had not helped matters by installing a candidate of his own, William Harrison Riley, to run the farm. Riley had been trying to interest Ruskin in co-operative ventures for some time; as a propagandist he edited a number of political journals, including the Sheffield *Socialist* for six months in 1877. Riley failed to please either Ruskin or the Totley workers, and in 1880 emigrated to America. Ruskin later said: 'of all the blackguards I ever came into collision with in my long life [Riley] was out and out the worst'.[20] Riley knew Edward Carpenter, and it was during the difficulties over the Totley farm that Ruskin and Carpenter corresponded. Finally Ruskin put someone reliable, his own gardener, David Downs in charge. The commune was abandoned, but Downs ran it successfully as a farm and market garden, and died there. The management passed to a former miner and quarry worker, George Pearson, who bought the house and land from the Guild in 1929. It is still there.

The narrative has taken us somewhat ahead of the visit of 1876, and the reader may be feeling in the mood reported by the *Sheffield Telegraph*: 'A majority of those present had evidently begun to tire of so much time being consumed by the subject of Communism; and art matters were introduced' (30.307). On this occasion Ruskin did not have a great deal to say on art matters, although he made some critical remarks about Holman Hunt's painting 'The Shadow of Death', a work that portrayed Jesus as a young carpenter in a pose that anticipates his crucifixion. It had been put on display in Sheffield at the Cutlers' Hall that March, with considerable popular success. The real art matter was the museum itself.

4. The 1884 extension to Walkley, with plaster casts from Venice in cases on the walls, Ruskin's study of Santa Maria della Spina, Pisa on an easel, and J.W. Bunney's painting of St Mark's behind.

As with St George's Farm, the reality was somewhat less than the ideal. One problem was the sheer lack of space. As the collection grew, with the acquisitions tracking Ruskin's shifting interests, notably his concern to record key elements of Venice, with plaster casts of sculpture and commissioned copies of mosaics and other works, the need to expand became urgent. In 1881 a plan to enlarge the Museum was replaced by a scheme to build on a new site at Endcliffe Gardens. There was considerable support for this locally, and funds were raised, but Ruskin had suffered his first mental breakdown in 1878, and from then on his control of the affairs of the Guild became intermittent, as attacks recurred. In 1884 a wooden extension was built on the back of the Walkley cottage, partly in order to house the large painting of the West Front of St Mark's that Ruskin had commissioned from John Bunney in 1877, and which he completed shortly before he died in 1882.

In 1885 Ruskin announced a totally new plan, to leave Walkley as it was, and build a museum on the land owned by the Guild at Bewdley, Worcestershire, but this came to nothing, partly because of lack of funds and partly Ruskin's failing mental health. Sheffield, evidently, was proud of the Ruskin connection however, and when the Corporation acquired Meersbrook House and Park in 1886, they suggested the Museum could move there. Ruskin was reluctant because of the question of who would own the collection and how it would be displayed, but by 1889 Ruskin had lost control of his affairs, and it was agreed that the Guild

5. The Mineral Room, Meersbrook Park. Ruskin's Venetian casts are on the walls, the minerals in the cabinets.

6. The Library, Meersbrook Park, with a quotation from Ruskin, as in the Mineral Room, on the frieze.

would lend the Corporation the collection, and the Corporation would house and display it in the Georgian house, adapted into a conventional picture gallery, with domestic accommodation for the curator.

Our last sight of the Walkley cottage – whose front façade survives as part of a much enlarged building, which at one time served as a refuge for 'fallen women' – comes once more from the *Sheffield Daily Telegraph*, this time on the occasion of the grand opening of Meersbrook Park. It is unlikely that it was the same reporter, but the writer seems to be anxious to promote the Corporation's civic generosity through this unflattering description of the old location:

> From the very first the Walkley site found little favour with the people . . . set amid squalid surroundings, and free from the slightest architectural adornment, the outer aspect of the building was forbidding – tolerable in summer, but bleak and cheerless in the months of winter. The truth must be told that the people for whom Ruskin had done so much refused to climb the painful slopes, flanked by unsightly blocks of bricks and mortar, to reach the little temple of art, and so gradually, but surely, came to be regarded as utterly inaccessible. Nor was that all. Within its humble walls the costly treasures were cribbed, cabined and confined, and either piled in neglected nooks or thrust into positions which robbed them of half their beauty. And in addition to this the place was beset with restrictions of a most irritating nature.[21]

* * *

21

Fortunately for Henry Swan, he had died before this was published, and indeed Swan's death in 1889 may have made the move to Meersbrook Park and larger premises possible. Although Ruskin never broke with Swan, his curator had a habit of exasperating him. When it looked in 1882 as though the Corporation of Sheffield was going to build him a new museum, Ruskin wrote to Joan Severn: 'The old place [Walkley] will not be sold, but become a centre of quaker St Georgism – which has its qualities – of a sort – The Swans will stay there – the curators of the new museum must be of another sort'.[22]

There is, however, a more friendly reminiscence of Walkley by the Reverend T.W. Holmes, describing a visit by Ruskin (the date is uncertain):

> I see the room just now as I saw it then. No common carrier or big furniture van can move to Meersbrook or elsewhere the ideal museum that exists in the study of my imagination. There they hang – the picture of the 'Storm at Sea' [by William Small] over the fireplace; Mr Ruskin's own drawing of the mountains, against the wall opposite the window; the delicately lovely water-colour of Coblentz, by the fireplace, the glorious opals, sapphires, emeralds, amethysts and agates, in the glass cases; the boxes near the door holding etchings by Dürer and other great masters; the piles of books in the corner of splendid paintings of insects, shells, fishes and birds; the magnificently bound books; the rare specimens of cloisonné enamelled vases (30.309).[23]

The most distinguished visitor to the museum in Swan's time was Prince Leopold, the youngest son of Queen Victoria, who had become a friend of Ruskin's in the 1870s when an undergraduate at Oxford, and was a Royal patron of the Ruskin School of Drawing. The half hour visit in October 1879, with Ruskin in attendance, was described at length in the *Sheffield and Rotherham Independent* (30.311-4), and we get a charming picture of Ruskin opening drawers and displaying specimens to the Prince. The reporter noted: '"I want", said [Ruskin], "to get everything beautiful"' (30.312).

And that, indeed, was one of the ruling motives behind the treasure trove that gradually accumulated: drawings, prints, photographs, coins, minerals and precious stones, a dozen illuminated manuscripts, printed books and collections of ornithological and botanical plates, furniture and Ruskin-designed display cases. When Ruskin was active the Guild acquisitions formed part of a bigger collection that circulated between his home at Brantwood, his rooms at Corpus Christi College in Oxford and the Drawing School, Whitelands teacher training college in Chelsea, Cheltenham Ladies College, Lady Margaret Hall and Somerville, fledging women's colleges at Oxford that he supported. When he lost control, some items ended up in the 'wrong' place, although to Ruskin it was all one. The core of the twenty or so artists in the collection came from the group of minor

English and Italian painters that Ruskin had employed – and often instructed by letter – to record works of art, flowers, landscape and buildings in France, Italy and Switzerland: J. W. Bunney, W. Hackstoun, Charles Fairfax Murray, T.M. Rooke, Frank Randal, H. R. Newman, H. Stacey Marks, Angelo Alessandri and Raffaelle Carloforti. (In 2002 the Guild acquired the Bunney family collection and archive, substantially increasing its holdings.)

Turner was represented by prints, and facsimiles by William Ward. Undoubtedly the most important work in the collection was 'The Madonna adoring the Infant Christ' by the 15th century master Andrea del Verocchio, in whose studio Leonardo da Vinci had worked. Ruskin acquired the tempera painting for £100 from the Manfrini collection in Venice in 1877, transferring it from its original wood panel to canvas and having it restored. Ruskin told Prince Leopold that the painting was the answer to the question he was often asked: 'What do you want to teach us about art?' (30.311-2).

Although not intended to encourage a specific skill, as in the case of the collection he assembled for his School of Drawing in Oxford, the Museum did have a broad educational purpose: 'it will have nothing in it but what deserves respect in Art, or admiration in Nature' (30.l). The substantial number of photographs, engravings, facsimiles, reproductions, chromolithographs and casts in the collection show that he saw it as a popular, working and teaching museum, where the exhibits could be handled, and the 'authenticity' of the object was less important than what it taught. At least two local artists were inspired by visits to the collection at Walkley: Benjamin Creswick, a Sheffield grinder who became a sculptor and taught at Birmingham School of Art, and the cabinet maker Frank Saltfleet, who rose to become President of the Sheffield Society of Artists. Ruskin never supplied his own complete catalogue, but the rich variety of materials, from art and nature, created a kind of self-portrait in this repository of his interests. An underlying theme was the museum as a form of conservation against the ravages of restoration. The 'memorial studies' (24.412) that he commissioned of St Mark's in Venice carry the melancholy suggestion that too much had already been lost.

It is evident from the descriptions that have been given that at Walkley the collection was, to say the least, informally displayed, but that is unlikely to have worried Ruskin a great deal, who believed in the oneness of things. A preliminary catalogue was drawn up by Henry Swan's son Howard in 1888. Swan's successor, William White was indeed 'of another sort', a professionally trained curator who had plenty of space to lay out the museum by subject matter. In 1890 White published *A Descriptive Catalogue of the Library and Print Room of the Ruskin*

Museum, and *The Principles of Art as illustrated by Examples in the Ruskin Museum at Sheffield; with passages, permission, from the writings of John Ruskin*, which provided a different kind of order by linking the works in the collection to quotations from Ruskin's voluminous writings on art. At Meersbrook the collection proved popular. 61,000 visitors were recorded in 1891-2, and averaged 45,000 a year before the First World War. White, and his successor in 1899 Gill Parker, ran an educational programme, with school visits, and there was also a Ruskin Club that met at the museum.

* * *

It is clear, however, that the Museum of the Guild of St George was only a sketch, a gesture towards the National Store of wealth that Ruskin described when outlining his own principles of Communism. If we look at his third principle again, where in the same sentence he speaks of: 'superb and precious things in redundant quantity, as pictures, statues, precious books ... and vast spaces of land for culture, exercise, and garden, round the cities' (27.121), we can see that the museum at Walkley and the farm at Totley were essentially indivisible in his mind, as were art and society.

Ruskin had enunciated the principle of the indivisibility of art and society long before he came to Sheffield, and when he described the principles upon which the Guild was to be founded his true source of ideas was not Communism as understood by the working men of Sheffield, but society as organised by the citizens of a very different city – Venice. When he talks of having only cheap, and few, pictures on the insides of houses where nobody but the owner can see them, but: 'costly pictures, and many, on the outsides of houses, where the people can see them' (27.120), he is plainly referring to Venice, where in the days of Titian, Giorgione and Veronese the walls of the palaces on the Grand Canal glowed with frescoes, frescoes of which but faded shreds remained in Ruskin's time.

The Guild of St George, as an *idea*, has more parallels with the *Scuole* of Venice than the English medieval trade guilds. The *Scuola* was a confraternity that was open to several ranks of citizens, and existed to perform both religious and charitable functions, while their chapels and meeting halls gave work to the great painters of Italy. Venice, though run by a closed oligarchy, was a republic, and it was the tradition that the great families devoted their wealth, not to the embellishment of private apartments, but the city as a whole. It is not surprising then, to find in *Fors Clavigera* for January 1877 Ruskin addressing the men who planned to work at Totley in these terms: 'Elect a doge, if, for the present, to act only as purveyor-general: honest doge, he must be, with an active and kind

24

duchess' (29.21). In the following month he holds out the idea that they may build themselves their own Ducal Palace, in Sheffield, one day.

It may be that it was the failure to elect a Doge, with his authority, that led to the squabbles at Totley. And after all, was not Ruskin himself, elected with absolute authority by the Companions, to be Doge of the Guild of St George? The link between Venice and Sheffield was made sadly real when Ruskin chose the museum as the repository for the casts, photographs, and studies of Venetian art and architecture that he acquired in an effort to preserve at least a record of the culture of a society threatened with destruction by the capitalist energies so profitably at work in Sheffield.

It is a long way from the Ducal Palace and the Venetian lagoon to thirteen acres of poor land at Totley and Walkley's single room. Yet we must come back to the twenty persons who came to hear Ruskin speak there. We must look on Ruskin's projects for the Guild of St George in a special way. Just as the vehicle for his ideas, *Fors Clavigera*, represented a distinctive way of arguing, so the practical (and impractical) schemes of the Guild were an extension of that argument. They were gestures, challenges, ways of getting people to act and think for themselves. Repeatedly, Ruskin states that his own duties lie elsewhere than in man-management, that he wants others to take the responsibility. The Guild's task was educational in the widest sense, of leading people towards a fuller recognition of themselves and their potential. It did not exist to make that realisation for them. That is why there is no coherent dogma or credo laid down for the Companions to obey, and it was to Ruskin's everlasting regret that while people were prepared to follow, few were ready to find their own way. In gently sardonic tones Ruskin wrote in *Fors Clavigera*: 'it would be a poor design indeed, for the bettering of the world, which any man could see either quite round the outside, or quite into the inside of' (28.235).

Ruskin's challenges did get responses, and his views on art and society, on the nature of work, on the need for education, and the damage we are doing to the environment are just as challenging in the 21st century as they were in the 19th. In the closing sentences of the anonymous *Sheffield Daily Telegraph* report Ruskin makes it clear that he is challenging us to respond to his ideas, – that it is up to us now, just as much as it was up to his audience then:

> The subject of the Museum was then discursively alluded to, Mr Ruskin stating that it is at present merely the nucleus of what he will make it if he finds that it is properly appreciated. In that event he would have works of the very best class, whether engravings, metal works, and other art objects.
>
> The discussion then closed, having lasted about three hours (30.309).

AFTERWORD

When I gave the original version of this lecture in the Mappin Art Gallery in 1979, the Museum of the Guild of St George was not displayed in the way it is today. The collection was not even in Sheffield, but languishing in much reduced circumstances at the University of Reading. The story of the later history of the Guild of St George is admirably told in James Dearden's *John Ruskin's Guild of St George* (2010)[24], but this account would not be complete without briefly bringing the history of the Museum up to date.

The Museum remained at Meersbrook Park under a series of loan agreements until 1953; William White's successor as curator, Gill Parker, serving as curator for thirty-two years, until 1931. But the Corporation of Sheffield found the upkeep of Meersbrook increasingly expensive, and after the end of the latest loan agreement the collection went into store, although selected items were shown in Sheffield's two public museums, the Graves and the Mappin. In 1954 Professor H.A. Hodges had become Master of the Guild; both he and his successor in 1973, Professor Cyril Tyler, were at Reading University. Coincidentally both art and agriculture were taught there. In 1963 it was decided to move the collection to Reading, where until 1972 much of the collection remained in a basement storeroom (where I saw it for the first time). In 1968 Dr Catherine Williams Morley was appointed a Research Fellow, and made a meticulous catalogue of the collection and a study of the Guild that was published as *John Ruskin, Late Work* (1984).[25] In 1969 Andrea Finn was appointed Curator.

After further scholarly work was done on the collection's chief treasure, Verrochio's 'The Madonna adoring the Infant Christ', which led to the suggestion that Leonardo may have contributed to the painting, the decision was taken to sell the picture, and in 1975 it was acquired by the National Galleries of Scotland, where it now remains. The sale was controversial among Ruskinians, but the money raised meant that the Guild could be much more active in promoting Ruskin's ideas. The arrangement with Reading University however was not very satisfactory. In 1977 Cyril Tyler resigned as Master, and pressure mounted for the collection to return to Sheffield.

In 1981 this was agreed, and plans were drawn up for an extension to be added to the Mappin Gallery. Unfortunately the Mappin is a listed building, and building consent was not given. The Corporation had another property, however, the former Hayes Wine Store in Norfolk Street in the city centre. (Since Ruskin's father had made his fortune as a sherry merchant, there was a certain appropriateness to taking over a vintner's.) In 1985, splendidly refurbished, and with new craft

7. The Ruskin Gallery in Norfolk Street, 1985-2001.

works commissioned, the Museum of the Guild of St George reopened as the Ruskin Gallery in Norfolk Street. A craft gallery also opened there in 1986. The Guild's collection was becoming better known, thanks to the Arts Council touring exhibition, *John Ruskin*, curated by Jeanne Clegg, which opened at the Mappin Gallery in 1983, and travelled to Liverpool, Kendal, and Oxford. In 1993, in association with the Accademia Italiana in London, the Guild supported *Ruskin and Tuscany*, curated by Jeanne Clegg and Paul Tucker, which was seen in Lucca and London as well as Sheffield. In 1996 Julian Spalding, a former curator for Sheffield museums service who had been one of the driving forces in bringing back the collection to Sheffield, and who was now running Glasgow's museums, became Master until 2005. In 1998 the Guild launched the Campaign for Drawing, which has since become an independent charity promoting the skill that Ruskin considered one of the fundamentals of all education.

In 2001, the collection moved again, this time to Sheffield's new Millennium Galleries. The display space was smaller than what was available in Norfolk

Street, and in order to give the collection more room to breathe it was decided that the Guild would promote a rolling programme of triennial exhibitions in the main Millennium Galleries, exploring Ruskinian themes and issues. The first opened in 2009, appropriately titled *Can Art Save Us?*

In March 2011 the Guild collection was redisplayed at the Millennium Galleries, in the form in which, at the time of writing, it can now be seen. It has travelled a long way since it first began to accumulate in that single crowded room in Henry Swan's cottage in Walkley.

NOTES

1. The report is reprinted, with slight variations, in *The Works of John Ruskin* (Library Edition), ed. E.T. Cook and A. Wedderburn, 39 vols., London, George Allen, 1903-1912, Vol. 30, pp. 306-309.

2. *The Sheffield Portrait Gallery*, November, 1875, p.6.

3. *The Works of John Ruskin*, Vol.29, p.197. All further references to the *Works* are included in the text by volume and page number, thus: (29.197).

4. Letter of G. Allen to J. W. Bunney, 20 February 1876, quoted by Dr C. Williams Morley in her catalogue to the Museum of the Guild of St George.

5. S. Rowbotham (with Jeffrey Weeks), *Socialism and the New Life*, London, Pluto Press, 1977, p.38.

6. [T. Hancock], "Henry Swan, The Quaker", *Pall Mall Gazette*, 3 April 1889.

7. W. Hargrave, "The Faithful Steward of the Ruskin Museum", *Pall Mall Gazette*, 2 April 1889.

8. In search of Henry Swan I consulted *The Phonograph: A Shorthand Literary Magazine*, published from July 1879 to March 1881 by M. Hurst, 23 Church Street, Sheffield. Unfortunately I was none the wiser, as it was all in shorthand. Swan's name, however, does not appear in the printed list of contributors.

9. Letter of G. Allen to John Hobbs, 26 April 1890, Pierpont Morgan Library, New York.

10. Typed transcript made for Cook and Wedderburn of letter from Ruskin to Tarrant and Mackrell, 27 September 1875. These transcripts are in the Bodleian Library, Oxford.

11. *Ibid.*

12. Typed transcript of a letter from Ruskin to G. Allen, 27 August 1875, Bodleian Library, Oxford.

13. *The Diaries of John Ruskin*, ed. Joan Evans and J.H. Whitehouse, 3 vols., Oxford University Press, 1956-59, Vol. 3, p.852.

14. The first two sentences of this quotation are taken from transcripts made by Helen Gill Viljoen from the correspondence between Ruskin and Swan held by the Rosenbach Foundation, Philadelphia. Viljoen continued the quotation in *The Brantwood Diary of John Ruskin,* ed. H.G. Viljoen, New Haven and London, Yale University Press, 1971, p.42n.

15. Autograph letter John Ruskin to Joan Severn, 26 September 1876, Ruskin Library, Lancaster University.

16. *The Diaries of John Ruskin*, *op.cit.*, Vol. 3, p.863.

17. *The Professor: Arthur Severn's Memoir of John Ruskin*, ed. J.S. Dearden, London, Allen & Unwin, 1967, p.88.

18. *The Letters of John Ruskin to Lord and Lady Mount-Temple*, ed. J.L. Bradley, Ohio State University Press, 1964, p.314. Letter of 4 August 1871.

[19] [David Robinson], "Political Economy", *Blackwood's Edinburgh Magazine*, Vol. 27 (January 1830), p.36.

[20] *The Brantwood Diary of John Ruskin*, op.cit., p.603.

[21] *Sheffield Daily Telegraph*, 14 April 1890.

[22] Autograph letter John Ruskin to Joan Severn, 25 July [1882], Ruskin Library, Lancaster University.

[23] T.W. Holmes "An Evening with Ruskin at Walkley" first appeared in *The Lamp; a Magazine for Christian Workers and Thinkers*, No. 1 (January 1892), pp. 13-17.

[24] J.S. Dearden, *John Ruskin's Guild of St George*, Bembridge, The Guild of St George, 2010

[25] Catherine Williams Morley, *John Ruskin, Late Work, 1870-1890: The Museum and the Guild of St George: An Educational Experiment*, New York, Garland, 1984.

KEEPERS AND CURATORS

1875-1889	Henry Swan
1890-1899	William White
1899-1931	Gill Parker
1931-1949	Genevieve Pilley (acting)
1949-1963	Richard Seddon
1969-1981	Andrea Finn
1982-1983	David Alston
1983-1995	Janet Barnes
1995-2001	Camilla Hampshire
2001-2009	Dorian Church
2004	Louise Pullen (Curator)
2009	Kim Streets (Keeper)

BY THE SAME AUTHOR:

John Ruskin: The Argument of the Eye, Thames & Hudson, Princeton University Press, 1976

Ruskin and Venice, Thames & Hudson, 1978 (as *Ruskin a Venezia*, Stamperia di Venezia, Venice, 1983)

Art and Society: Ruskin in Sheffield, 1876, The Guild of St George Ruskin Lecture 1979, Brentham Press,1979 (appeared in Japanese translation, Wild Olives Group, Yokohama, 1990)

New Approaches to Ruskin: Thirteen Essays, (editor) Routledge, 1981

The Ruskin Art Collection at Oxford; The Rudimentary Series, (editor) Lion & Unicorn Press, Royal College of Art, 1984

Ruskin and Oxford: The Art of Education, Oxford University Press, 1996

Ruskin's Venice, Pilkington Press, 2000

Ruskin's Artists: Studies in the Victorian Visual Economy, (editor) Ashgate, 2000

Ruskin, Turner and the Pre-Raphaelites, catalogue of the Tate Centenary Exhibition, with Ian Warrell and Stephen Wildman, Tate Gallery Publications, 2000

An Address Delivered in St Andrew's Church, Coniston, on the Centenary of the Death of John Ruskin, privately printed by the Cygnet Press for the Ruskin Association, 2003

John Ruskin, (VIP no.10) Oxford University Press, 2007

Of Ruskin's Gardens, The Guild St George Ruskin Lecture 2009, The Guild of St George, 2009

Ruskin on Venice: 'The Paradise of Cities', Yale University Press, 2010